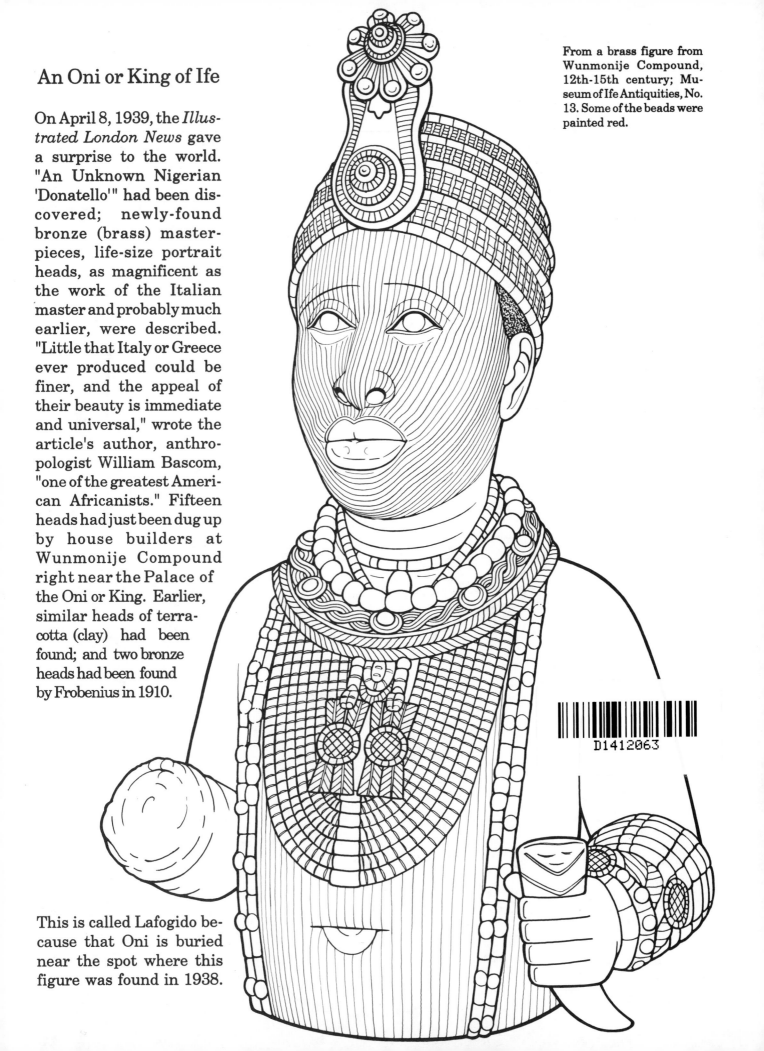

An Oni or King of Ife

On April 8, 1939, the *Illustrated London News* gave a surprise to the world. "An Unknown Nigerian 'Donatello'" had been discovered; newly-found bronze (brass) masterpieces, life-size portrait heads, as magnificent as the work of the Italian master and probably much earlier, were described. "Little that Italy or Greece ever produced could be finer, and the appeal of their beauty is immediate and universal," wrote the article's author, anthropologist William Bascom, "one of the greatest American Africanists." Fifteen heads had just been dug up by house builders at Wunmonije Compound right near the Palace of the Oni or King. Earlier, similar heads of terracotta (clay) had been found; and two bronze heads had been found by Frobenius in 1910.

From a brass figure from Wunmonije Compound, 12th-15th century; Museum of Ife Antiquities, No. 13. Some of the beads were painted red.

This is called Lafogido because that Oni is buried near the spot where this figure was found in 1938.

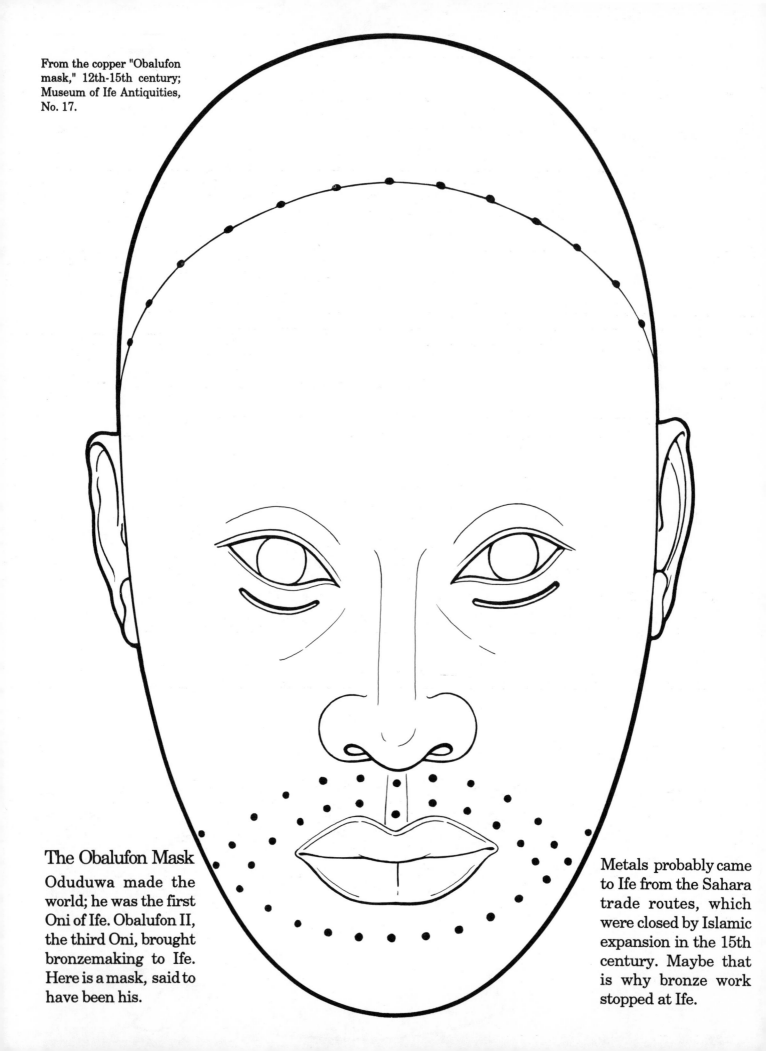

From the copper "Obalufon mask," 12th-15th century; Museum of Ife Antiquities, No. 17.

The Obalufon Mask

Oduduwa made the world; he was the first Oni of Ife. Obalufon II, the third Oni, brought bronzemaking to Ife. Here is a mask, said to have been his.

Metals probably came to Ife from the Sahara trade routes, which were closed by Islamic expansion in the 15th century. Maybe that is why bronze work stopped at Ife.

From a brass group found at Ita Yamoo in 1957; Museum of Ife Antiquities. The beads on his crown, and both their neck beads and garments were painted red. The queen's crown and hair were painted black.

Ife ondaiye, ibi oju ti imo wa—Ife, the creator of the world, whence comes the light.

An Oni and Queen

The Onis of Ife were the overlords of the Obas or Kings of Benin, whose gorgeous bronzes may be seen in another Bellerophon Book. When Europeans appeared at Benin in 1485, they noted that the Obas there sent presents to the Onis of Ife, who in return sent back presents made of brass. Bronze work had been ongoing in Ife well before the arrival of Europeans.

Anthropologist Bascom took two of the bronze figures back to the United States. Soon he became a very famous professor, and the heads went with him to the University of California, in Berkeley. But the then Oni became upset, and British functionaries in Nigeria, Murray and Duckworth, joined in the clamoring to have the heads returned. Good Professor Bascom gave his two heads back to the Oni, who had just built a nice museum for them. But another bronze head had gone to the British Museum. Although the British growled at the Americans for wanting such great art, they did not even consider sending back their priceless head. You can see the returned heads on the covers.

From a brass head from Wunmonije Compound, 12th-15th century; Museum of Ife Antiquities, No. 19.

From a copper head, 12th-15th century; from Wun-monije Compound, found in 1939; Museum of Ife Antiquities, No. 6.

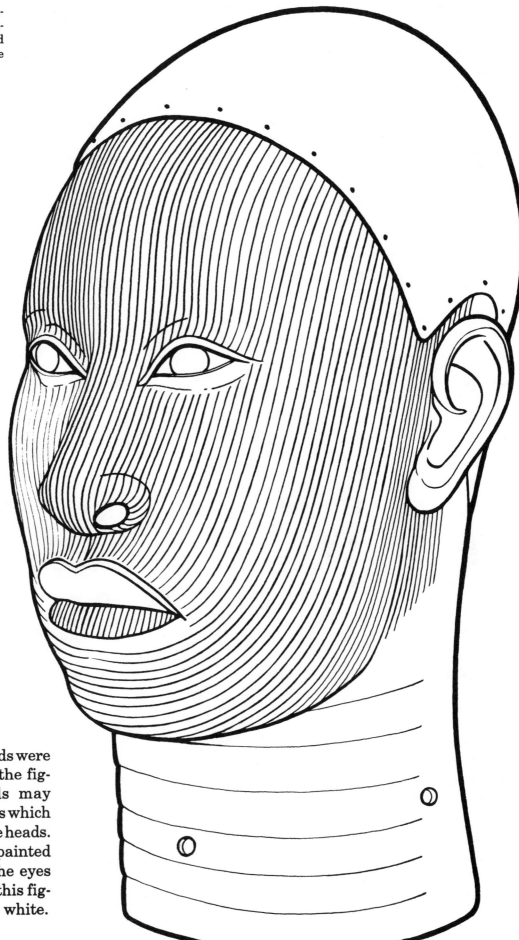

Beautiful glass beads were often dug up with the figures. These beads may have been on crowns which were attached to the heads. Lines of red were painted above and below the eyes and on the neck of this figure. The eyes were white.

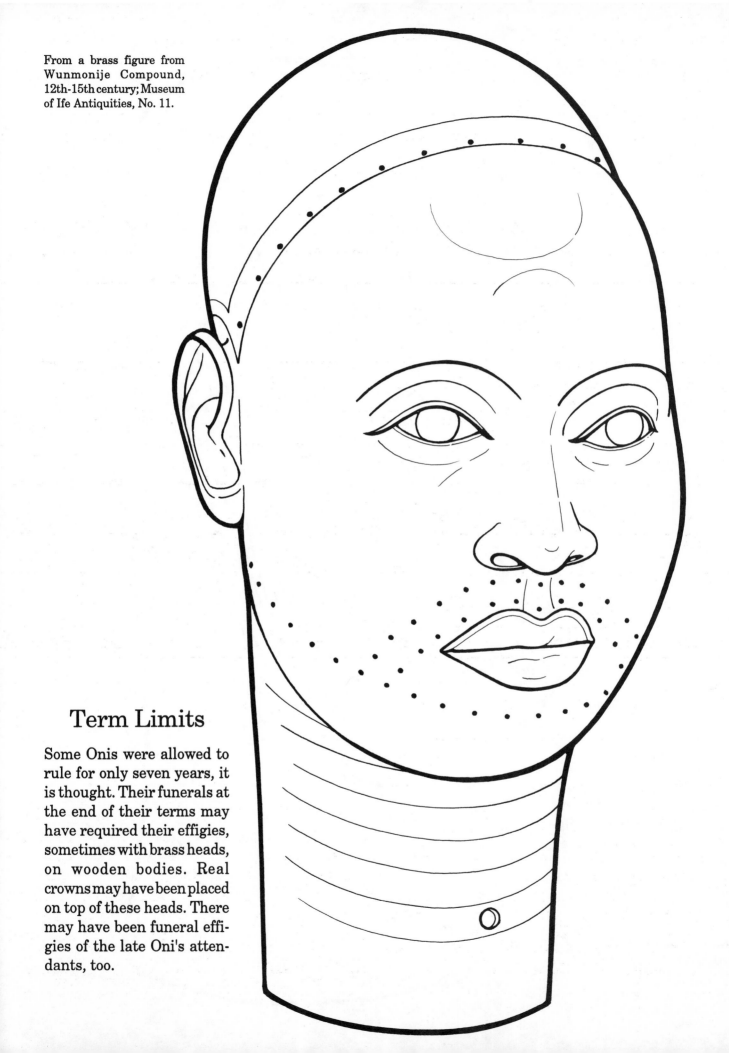

Term Limits

Some Onis were allowed to rule for only seven years, it is thought. Their funerals at the end of their terms may have required their effigies, sometimes with brass heads, on wooden bodies. Real crowns may have been placed on top of these heads. There may have been funeral effigies of the late Oni's attendants, too.

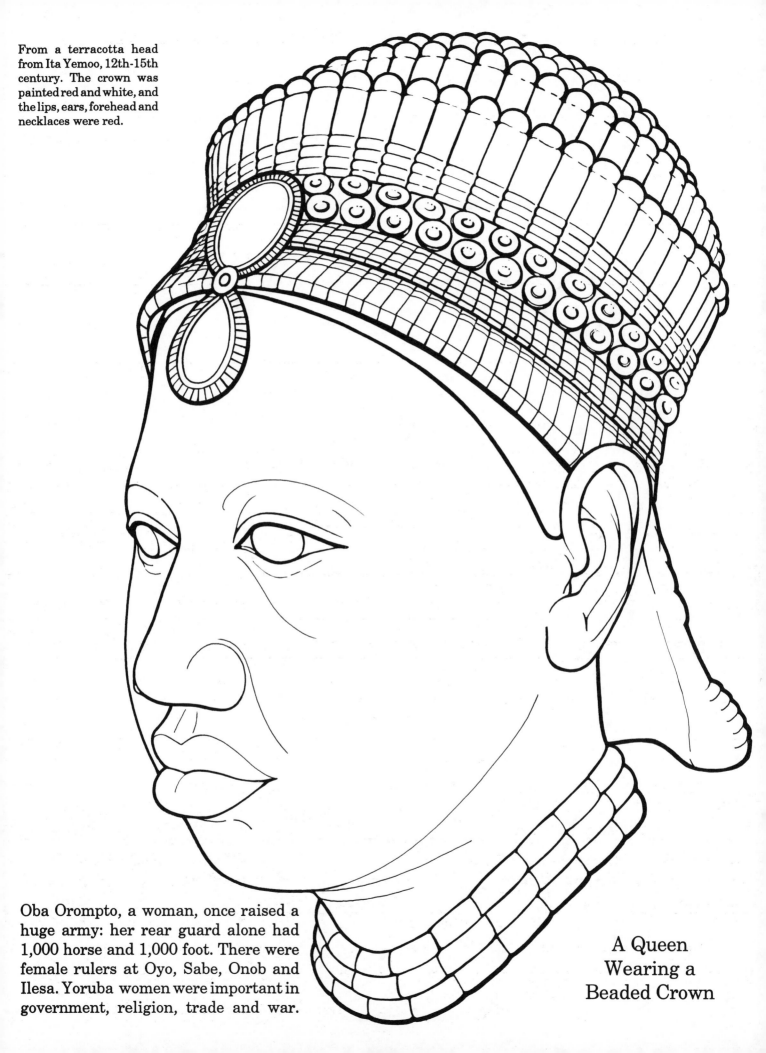

From a terracotta head from Ita Yemoo, 12th-15th century. The crown was painted red and white, and the lips, ears, forehead and necklaces were red.

Oba Orompto, a woman, once raised a huge army: her rear guard alone had 1,000 horse and 1,000 foot. There were female rulers at Oyo, Sabe, Onob and Ilesa. Yoruba women were important in government, religion, trade and war.

A Queen Wearing a Beaded Crown

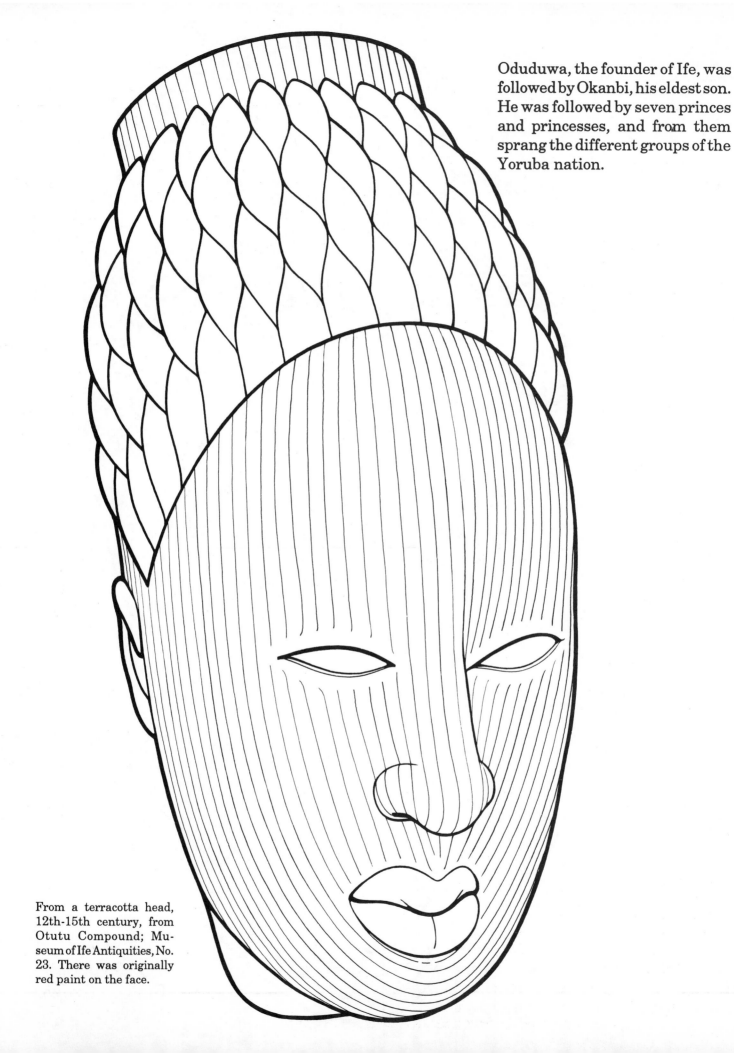

Oduduwa, the founder of Ife, was followed by Okanbi, his eldest son. He was followed by seven princes and princesses, and from them sprang the different groups of the Yoruba nation.

From a terracotta head, 12th-15th century, from Otutu Compound; Museum of Ife Antiquities, No. 23. There was originally red paint on the face.

Oranyan, Oduduwa's youngest son, later became Alafin, or King of all Kings, at Ife, the original capital of the Yoruba people. He founded Oyo, which became the most powerful Yoruba kingdom. The Kings of the other groups descended from Oranyan and Oduduwa.

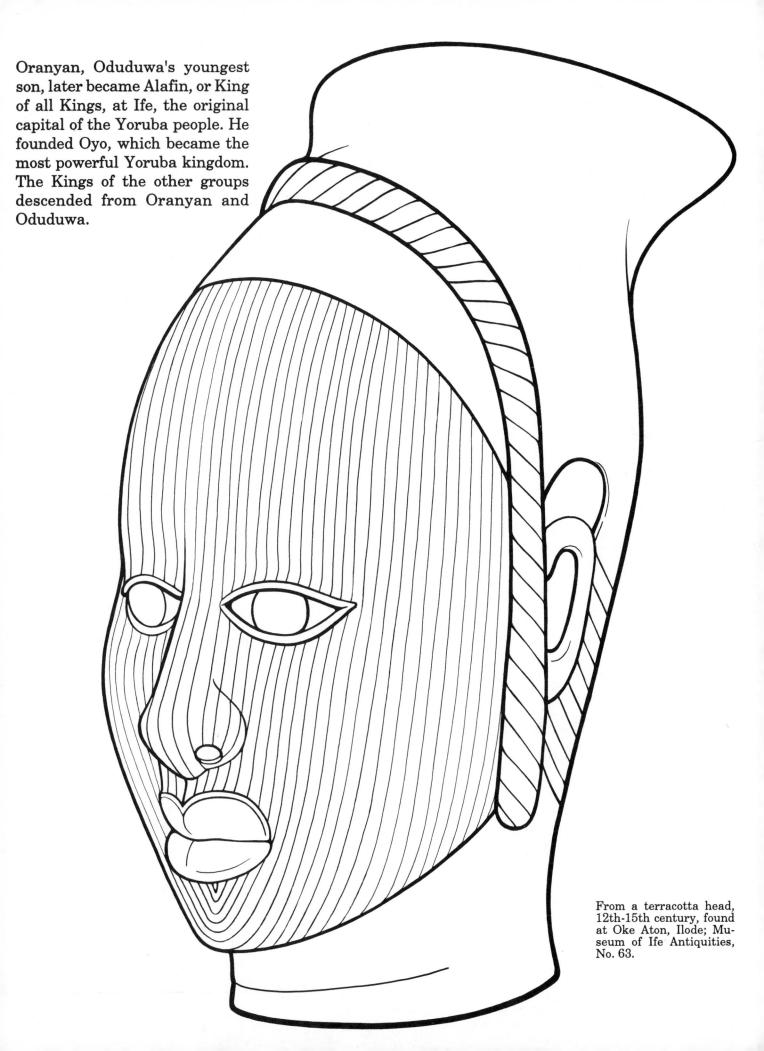

From a terracotta head, 12th-15th century, found at Oke Aton, Ilode; Museum of Ife Antiquities, No. 63.

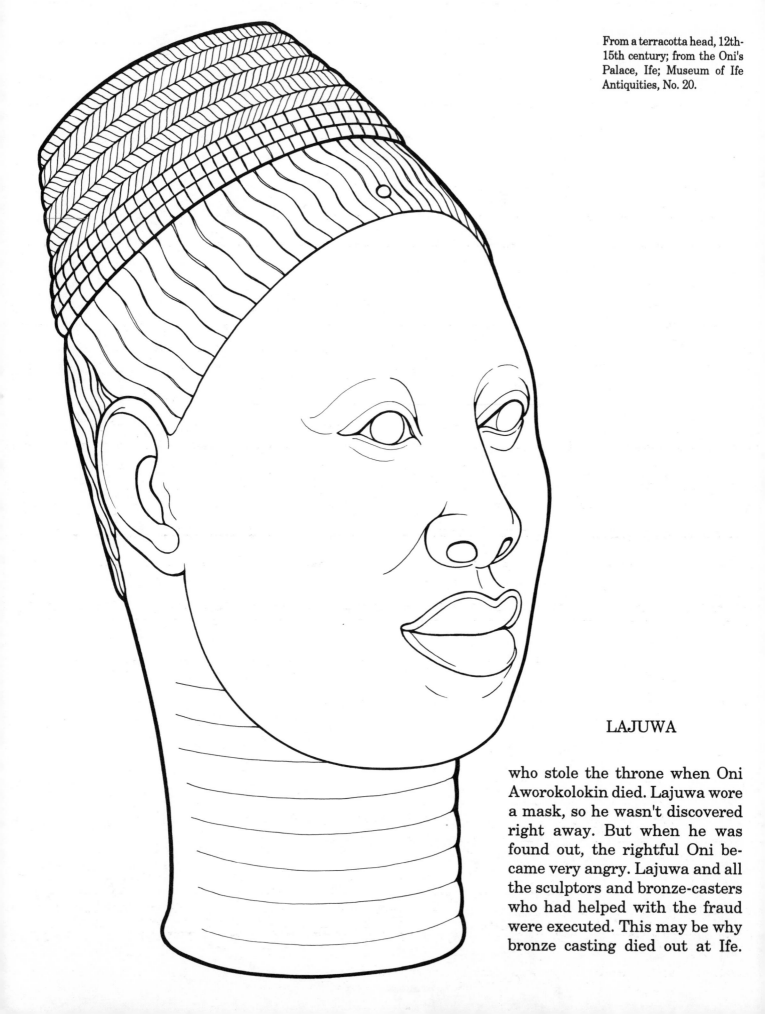

From a terracotta head, 12th-15th century; from the Oni's Palace, Ife; Museum of Ife Antiquities, No. 20.

LAJUWA

who stole the throne when Oni Aworokolokin died. Lajuwa wore a mask, so he wasn't discovered right away. But when he was found out, the rightful Oni became very angry. Lajuwa and all the sculptors and bronze-casters who had helped with the fraud were executed. This may be why bronze casting died out at Ife.

From a terracotta head, 12th-
15th century; from Odo Ogbe
Street, Ife; National Museum,
Lagos, No. 73.

The Alafin was the supreme
head of all the Kings. Curious
ceremonies were performed before his coronation. He ate a dish
made from the late King's heart.
At his coronation he worshiped at
the tombs of his ancestors, from
whom he received permission to
wear the crown. Afterwards he
went to the tomb of Sango, an
early King, for the crowning. Then
he went to the shrine of Oranyon
to receive the Sword of Justice
from Ife; he could not order exe-
cutions without it. Then he went
to the shrine of Ogun, the war
god, to ask for a peaceful reign.
Calabashes were brought from
Ife, and were used to divine what
would happen in the new reign.

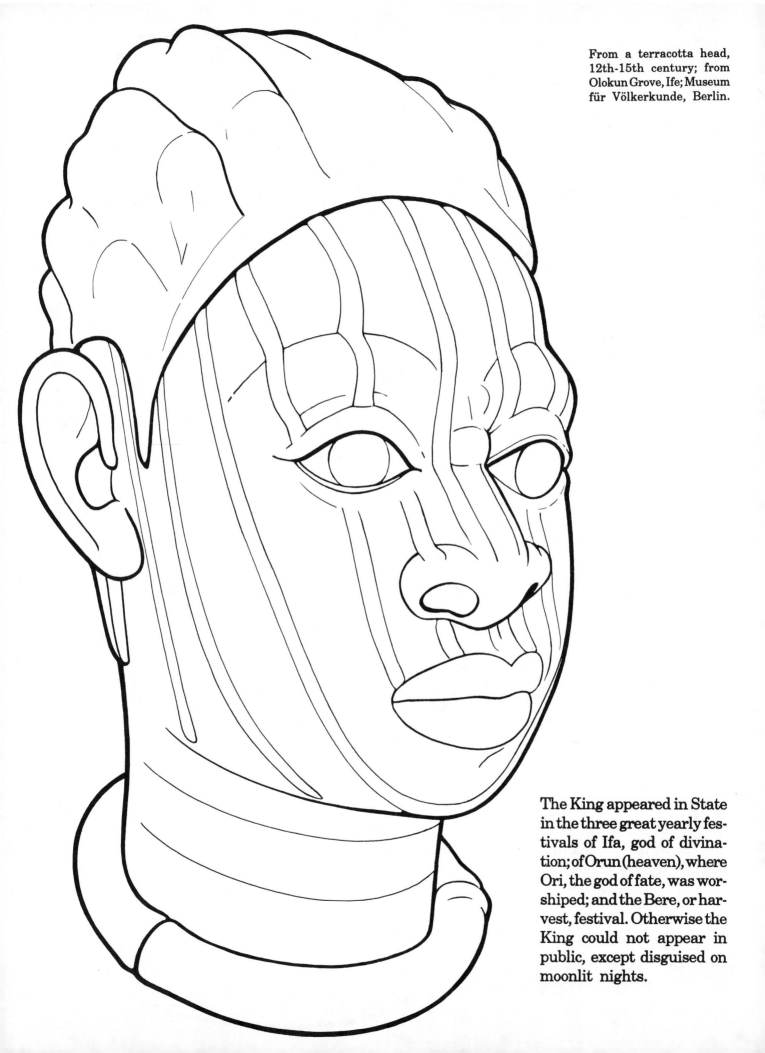

From a terracotta head, 12th-15th century; from Olokun Grove, Ife; Museum für Völkerkunde, Berlin.

The King appeared in State in the three great yearly festivals of Ifa, god of divination; of Orun (heaven), where Ori, the god of fate, was worshiped; and the Bere, or harvest, festival. Otherwise the King could not appear in public, except disguised on moonlit nights.

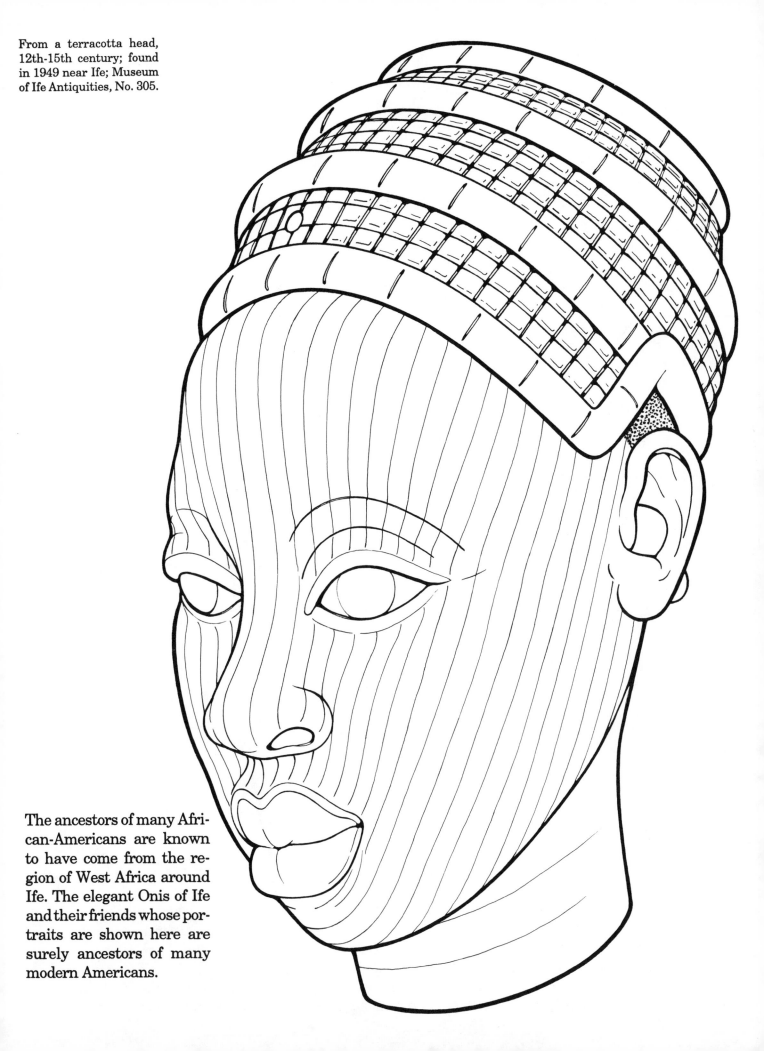

From a terracotta head, 12th-15th century; found in 1949 near Ife; Museum of Ife Antiquities, No. 305.

The ancestors of many African-Americans are known to have come from the region of West Africa around Ife. The elegant Onis of Ife and their friends whose portraits are shown here are surely ancestors of many modern Americans.

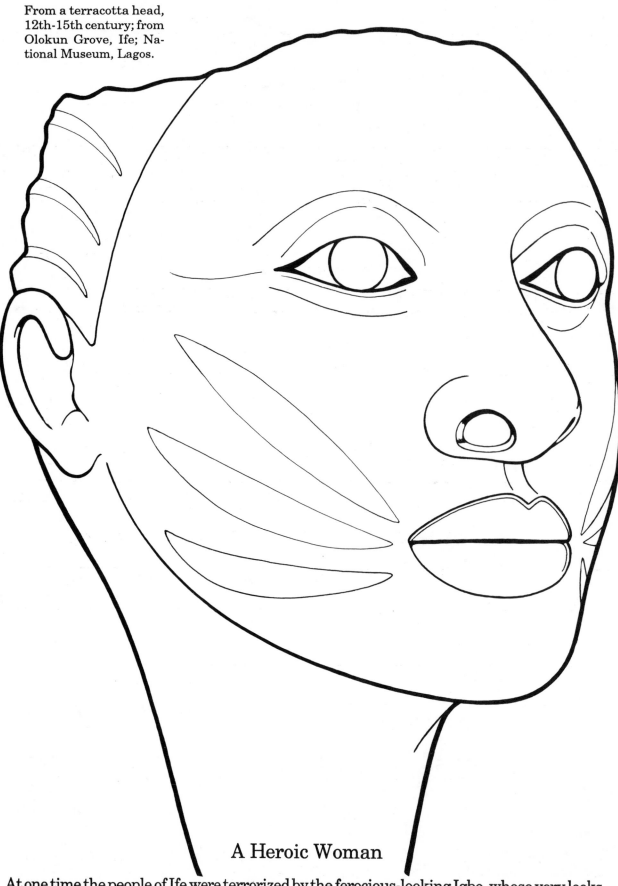

From a terracotta head, 12th-15th century; from Olokun Grove, Ife; National Museum, Lagos.

A Heroic Woman

At one time the people of Ife were terrorized by the ferocious-looking Igbo, whose very looks were so scary that the Ife didn't even try to resist them. The Igbo burned up Ife and captured Moremi, a beautiful Ife woman. Soon the King of the Igbo became very fond of her. Moremi learned that the Igbo were really just ordinary people, and that they looked fierce only because of their war costumes of raffia. Moremi managed to escape; she told the Ife they could fight the Igbo and their combustible outfits with fire. Soon the Ife were victorious.

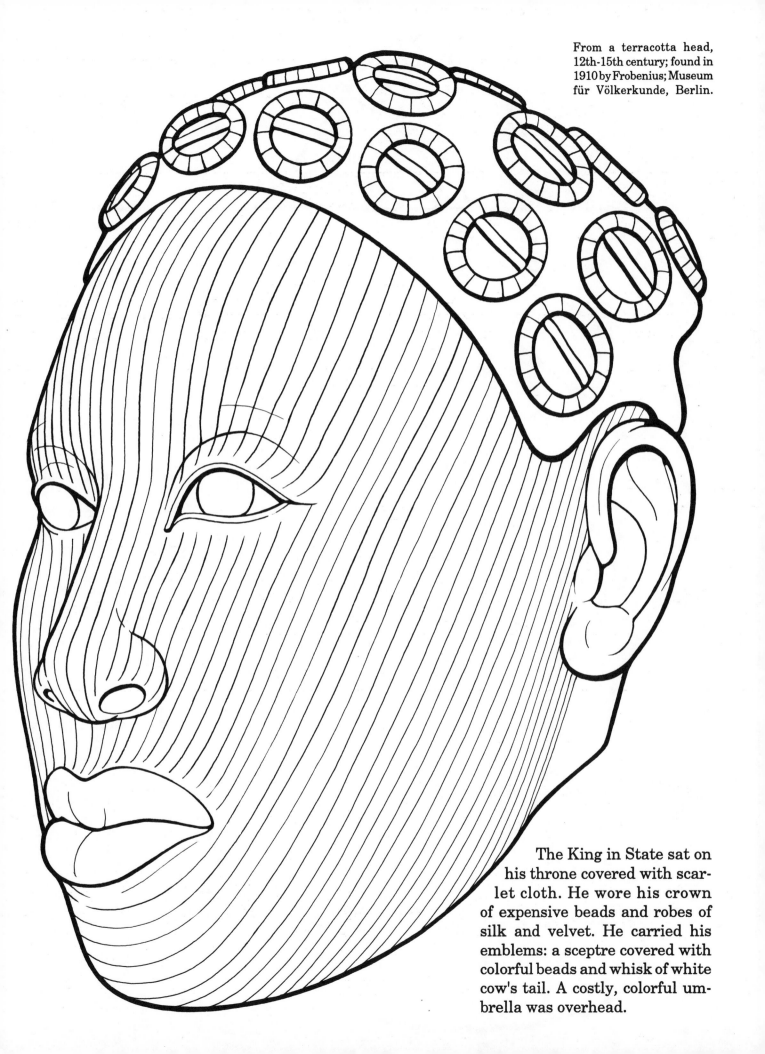

From a terracotta head, 12th-15th century; found in 1910 by Frobenius; Museum für Völkerkunde, Berlin.

The King in State sat on his throne covered with scarlet cloth. He wore his crown of expensive beads and robes of silk and velvet. He carried his emblems: a sceptre covered with colorful beads and whisk of white cow's tail. A costly, colorful umbrella was overhead.

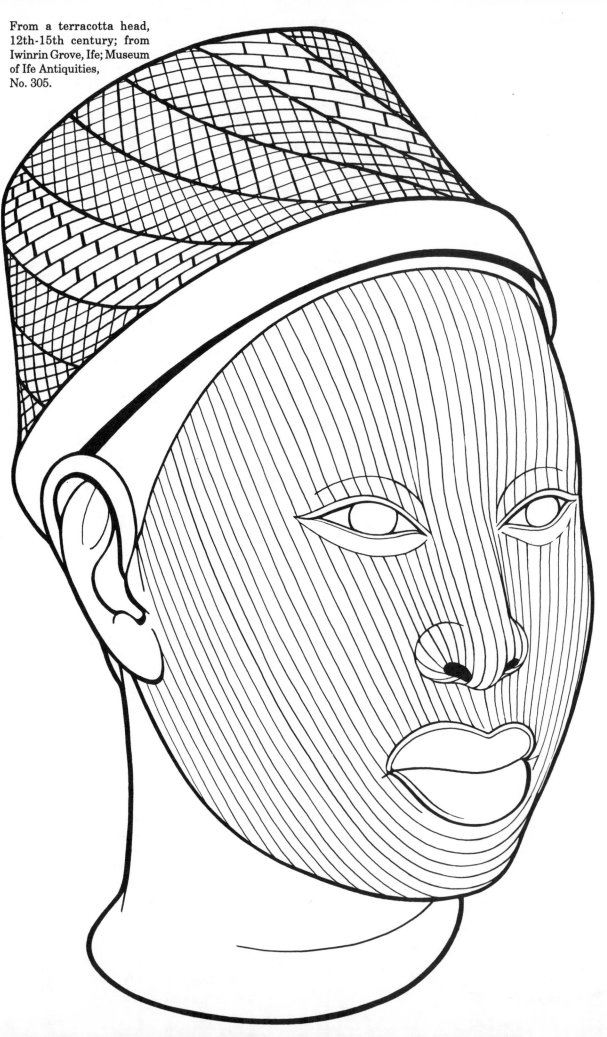

From a terracotta head, 12th-15th century; from Iwinrin Grove, Ife; Museum of Ife Antiquities, No. 305.

All of the Obas of Benin were said to have been descended from Oni Oronmiyon of Ife. When an Oba died, his head was sent to Ife for burial, and from there a bronze head was sent back to Benin. One day it was suggested that it would be easier if a bronze-smith were sent from Ife to Benin, to teach the Beni how to do this marvelous work. Oba Oguola of the 14th century sent Igueghae as a teacher to Benin. He did his job well. And from this we can learn that bronze making was established at Ife in the 14th century.